Cunning Spells

Table of Contents

I. INTRODUCTION & FOREWORD - PAGES 8 TO 11

II. MANDATORY ADMONITIONS: DISCLAIMER - PAGE 12
HISTORY - PAGES 13 TO 14
PROTECTION - CHAPTER 1 - PAGES 15 TO 17
MANIFESTATION - CHAPTER 2 - PAGES 18 TO 20
WHERE TO START - CHAPTER 3 - PAGES 21 TO 24

III. THE CORE SPELLS
DOMINATION SPELLS - CHAPTER 4 - PAGES 25 TO 27
CURSES & HEXES (DEFENCE) - CHAPTER 5 - PAGES 28 TO 30
BANISHING - CHAPTER 6 - PAGES 31 TO 34
EXORCISMS - CHAPTER 7 - PAGES 35 TO 37
LOVE SPELLS - CHAPTER 8 - PAGES 38 TO 40
CURSES - CHAPTER 9 - PAGES 41 TO 44
DEMONIC ATTACK - CHAPTER 10 - PAGES 45 TO 47
DEATH SPELLS - CHAPTER 11 - PAGES 48 TO 50
FUNNY SPELLS - CHAPTER 12 - PAGES 51 TO 53

IV. ADVANCED RECIPES & CONCISE COMMANDS 54 SPELLS 24 - 66
OTHER SPELLS - CHAPTER 13 - PAGES 54 TO 77
A. AGGRESSIVE DEFENSE AND COUNTER - COMMAND SPELLS 24 - 28
B. SEIZURE OF FORTUNE AND DOMINATION OF INFLUENCE SPELLS 29 - 38
C. EXTREME DOMINATION AND AUTHORITY SPELLS 39 - 43
D. JUSTICE, COURT CASES, AND LEGAL SUBVERSION SPELLS 44 - 47
E. PERMANENT BANISHING AND REMOVAL SPELLS 48 – 51
F. RETRIBUTION AND SEALING SPELLS 52 - 55
G. MANIPULATIVE LUST AND UNBREAKABLE BINDING SPELLS 56 - 59
H. CURSES, HEXES, AND SPIRITUAL ATTACKS SPELLS 60 - 64
I. PETTY AND VENGEFUL MAGICK SPELLS 65 - 66
THE END - PAGE 78
CASE FILES - CHAPTER 14 - PAGES 79 TO 84

Copyrights & Trademarks

PERMISSION MAY BE GRANTED TO REPRODUCE OR COPY THIS WORK BUT YOU MUST SEEK PERMISSION FROM Madame Verveine of BeWitchy.
support@bewitchy.com

Published by BeWitchy
© 2026 by Luan Heslin/Madame Verveine. All rights reserved.
No part of this book may be reproduced in any form or by any electronic or mechanical means, including information storage and retrieval systems, without written permission from the author, except for the use of brief quotations in a book review.

If you find this book, pdf or digital copies of this book online, it was most likely done without permission.
Please report it to violations@bewitchy.com

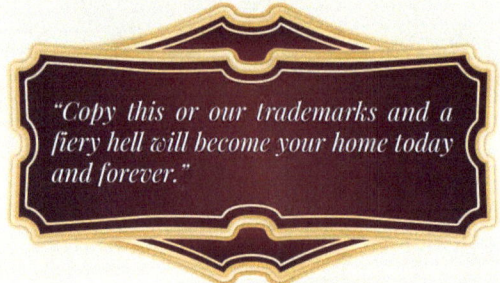

"Copy this or our trademarks and a fiery hell will become your home today and forever."

66 Black Magick Spells

Here within lies
66 Black Magic Spells
or variations of.

How dark you want to make
them all depends on your
own desires and needs.

Take Care
Be Aware
& Don't Do Anything
I Wouldn't Do! (witches cackle)...

Introduction

I first thank my "Black" mum (who carried the Balkan bloodline, though some might consider her brown - Americans used to call dark skinned Germans Black Dutch), Anne (Annie or Anitsa), who was taken from us all too soon. In a dark and horrible way that she and I once predicted for her. An avoidable act, who would ever have thought!

She was my biggest ally. My biggest difficulty. And my biggest love. She was often misunderstood. Often disliked by some for her tremendous honesty.

She taught me less with words and more by simply allowing me to observe her life. She gifted me the "sight"—the raw ability to watch, learn from her mistakes, and navigate a colourful life full of ups and downs. I fast became a thinker, an observer. And she also gifted me the other kind of "sight" - the ability to read someone like a book without them even uttering a word.

Her explanations were often "lathered in sailoring words"—in other words, she swore a lot. A simple instruction like, "no, don't do it that way" often came out as, "don't be so fucking stupid!"

This communication style—which some might call abuse—actually gave me perspective. I believe it prepped me for the dark world we live in. She was the woman who allowed a four-year-old me to watch many séances, who opened the door to the paranormal, and who always believed. She was the one who taught me witchcraft and manifestation, crossing out the faces of those who threatened her happiness.

I am forever grateful to my mum. Other kids used to make fun of my white skin or even her darker skin. We often joked that I was "white on the outside and black on the inside." Perhaps it was not far from the truth.

Whilst she was not a perfect mum (there is a dark complicated element to this life we had), who of us is... Sometimes I forget you are gone from this world.

Introduction

To my three magnificent children: Brock, my eldest, and his possession of a rigid sense of humor that always keeps me guessing. Your magnificent quirks keep me on my toes, especially your seemingly skeptical jokes—like asking if I'm doing voodoo again when I light incense. Thank you for your patience and for allowing me to live, grow, and do what I needed to do as your single mum. I love being your mother more than you could ever know, and I was devastated the day you moved out. But alas I did no voodoo on you and let you be you...

Ava, oh Ava. A true gifted psychic medium, like her mum since a small child. This girl is mind-blowing! I've known and worked with many "psychics," and none compare to the little rock you are. Thank you for loving me with all your heart and being there for me. You can do anything you set your mind to, you are multi-talented (like your mum) and you've already surpassed me with your constant gift-giving and talents. You are greater than you realize, and you will rule the world, given a moment. Seize opportunities, make your own, and never give up on a desire! I love that you admire me and are "obsessed" with me. I love you too, xo.

Willow, Willow, Willow, with your sweetest, kindest nature and your fire. You keep me grounded, reminding me of what is important: love, life, and family. You are the purest of heart, showing everyone love and care, and I hope you hold onto that forever. I wish you all the best and know you will manifest the truest desires of your pure heart, mind, and soul. And wow, can you sing and dance! Please do not ever give that up!

Many loves and bits and bobs to you all.

To my Husband: You were a little taken aback when we started this life together. I laugh at the memory of you pulling a face every time I smudged, knowing something was going down. But you were no stranger to the paranormal, and your open-mindedness allowed me to express myself openly, accepting me to be as "evil and as bad" as I wanted to be.

It takes one hell of a man to be able to do that and put up with my work-aholic chaotic, mad as fuck vibes!

Thank you for supporting my growth, spirituality, and witchcraft when others would have scoffed and judged and disliked or been terrorfied. Thank you for giving me the freedom and time to do what I needed and wanted. xx

Introduction

Who is Madame Verveine? I am an Entrepreneur, a Natural Born Psychic Medium, Clairvoyant, Demonologist, and more. With all gift aspects, there is truly no area I cannot read or see. I am a self-appointed High Priestess and Boo!jee Ass Witch, Artist, Musician, Producer, Author, and Graphic Designer (amongst other things).

I own a number of businesses, including, but not limited to: BeWitchy, BeWitchy LLC, The Tarot Witch, The Sex Psychic, The Seer, and Ghetto Witch plus more. I am in the know, legit, and genuine. I am a truth teller, mind-blowingly accurate, a Mentor to many, and, of course, a comedian with my dark sense of humor and quick wit. I know everything I know naturally and without haste, and it has never been wrong.

I support my clients by giving them the knowledge, insight, and tools to live their fullest, most stable, and happiest lives—something many other so-called "readers" could learn to do. The problem is that many are just jumping on bandwagons, not truly gifted, driven by ego and a desire to be god-like.

I am a straight shooter. We all have intuition, and we are all capable of listening and using it to our advantage. You were given it from birth for a reason, and you should fucking listen to it! But that doesn't mean everyone is meant to be a gifted psychic medium reader—that is often just sales talk and bullshit.

Things are not what they used to be, and it is true that social media and the internet have impacted our lives and fucked us hard like a porcupine eating a watermelon. There is no remorse, no reprieve, and we must make our lives the best that we can given these funked-up mouldy lemons called our technological-based lives.

You're probably wondering what gives me the right to be so opinionated or judgy with respect some of this and the truth is, it's because I am very good at what I do, I am in the know, it means a lot to me (I am passionate about it and highly ethical) and I thrive on honesty. Any client who has ever been to me can tell you that. Sure I am not the bearer of white light or bringer of all things nice, but I tell the truth, get the job done and can give a client all aspects—i.e. what will happen if they do this and what will happen if they do that... I share the survival tools required to assist.

Unlike the Charlatans that live amongst us, I give my clients real help, tools to not just survive but thrive! Succeed and find happiness!

Foreword

You are not reading some dusty academic text written by someone who uses magick as a hobby. This is a Cunning Magick manual written by someone who stands by the results.

I don't deal in "love and light" fluff. If you are here, you need results. You need a person gone, a debt paid, an obstacle crushed, or an enemy put in their place. This book will teach you how to claim your power and command the universe to deliver what you demand.

This is a book for the unapologetic, the fierce, and the Boo!jee Ass Witches of the world who know their worth and refuse to compromise. Read every word. Study every spell. Do not skip the protection work. Your power is waiting.

Madame Verveine
High Priestess and Witch

Disclaimers

MANDATORY ADMONITIONS: A NOTE TO THE PRACTITIONER

This text, the Cunning Magick Compendium, is not intended for casual curiosity or light experimentation. By engaging with these instructions, the practitioner acknowledges and agrees to the following immutable conditions:

I. ON MATTERS OF FAITH AND LEGAL SOVEREIGNTY

The spells, rituals, and philosophical tenets contained within this work are presented as an expression of sacred, faith-based practice rooted in the traditions of the Left-Hand Path and various forms of assertive, self-serving, and command-based spiritual belief.

- **Legal Standing:** The contents of this compendium are intended purely for spiritual, religious, and philosophical exploration. We assert the protection of faith and religious freedom for the practices described herein. The practitioner uses these methods entirely at their own risk and must be fully aware that specific actions, interpretations, or outcomes resulting from these beliefs may be subject to legal scrutiny in various jurisdictions. The author and publisher bear no responsibility for any legal action, civil or criminal, taken against the practitioner.
- **Ethical Autonomy:** This text assumes the practitioner possesses full ethical autonomy and personal responsibility for the intention and consequence of their actions. The Compendium is a tool for the dominant will, not a guide for the naive.

II. PREREQUISITE KNOWLEDGE AND SKILL REQUIREMENT
THIS IS NOT A BOOK FOR BEGINNERS. PROCEED AT YOUR OWN RISK.

The instructions within this Compendium are written with the understanding that the practitioner already possesses a solid foundational knowledge base in the Cunning Arts. This includes, but is not limited to:

1. **Celestial Mechanics:** A working knowledge of lunar phases, solar timing, and planetary hours.
2. **Basic Energetic Work:** The ability to raise and direct personal power without external aids.
3. **Hoodoo/Folk Magick Fundamentals:** Familiarity with common materia magica, including but not limited to basic powders (e.g., Goofer Dust, Hot Foot Powder), oils, and root work.

If the practitioner is not fluent in these foundational disciplines, the spells contained within this book will not only fail but may also lead to unintended, uncontrolled, or adverse spiritual consequences. The Compendium provides the advanced command structure, not the elementary education. The user assumes all risk for proceeding without adequate prior expertise.

History:
The Root of Cunning Magick

To Wield the Dark
To wield the dark, you must understand the shadow.
There is a lot of noise out there about what Black Magic is. Is it Satanic? Is it just for the "evil"? Let's cut the crap.

What is Black Magic?
Essentially, it is any form of magic used to restrict or mess with the free will of another. Whether you are cursing someone to financial ruin, summoning negative energy, or manipulating them into loving you, if you are bending the natural order to your will, you are walking the darker path.

But let's look at the timeline. We can only go back as far as the written word allows, but the truth is, this has been happening since the beginning of time—as soon as anyone had the gusto to work it out. If Adam and Eve were dumb enough to eat the fruit God told them not to, was that not the original act of defiance? The original "do as thou wilt?"

The Roots of the Craft
While I could sit here and quote articles from the 1100s or discuss the Maleficia of the Middle Ages, the roots go deeper. We are talking about the lead curse tablets dropped into Roman wells, the binding spells of Ancient Egypt, and the invocation of spirits in Babylon. From Necromancy (death magic) to Pyromancy (fire) and Demonology, the "dark arts" have always existed under different names.

Historically, much of this wasn't kept in writing because the partakers didn't want to be killed for practicing it. It was hidden in the shadows, passed down through whispers. It is a shame, really, as I am sure we would have benefited from that lost knowledge. Instead, history is often written by the victors—usually the religious institutions that labeled anything they couldn't control as "Devil Worship."

The Cunning Tradition
This brings us to where I stand. I prefer the term Cunning Magick. This isn't a modern invention; it is the raw, results-driven practice that pre-dates the sanitized, commercialized version of witchcraft you see today. The Cunning Witch didn't worry about the ethics of the Fae or the alignment of the planets; they worried about survival.

- Protection: Warding against the evil eye or a curse from a rival family.
- Healing: Removing illness or spiritual affliction.
- Offence: Placing a curse on a thief, a cheat, or a romantic rival.
- Fortune: Drawing money, love, or luck to a struggling business.

History:
The Root of Cunning Magick

The Lie of Ownership
I am now going to say something that others are too afraid to say: No person, culture, or colour OWNS magic or its practices. Although I wholeheartedly respect the need to protect it, honor its origins, and keep it real (i.e., true to its original form), everyone has the right to adopt any practice into their own. However, it should be done with respect, recognizing its roots and not changing something up and pretending it is your own. If you have adapted it, be honest about that. Call it something else and or again, credit it's origins.

We live in a social media world of "opinionates," bullies, and fear-mongers who claim that if you haven't been initiated into a specific lineage, the spirits will strike you down. That is a load of shit and nothing but scare tactics. It's the pagan equivalent of a preacher telling you that you're going to hell—rather hypocritical, isn't it?

Yes, acknowledge where something originated. Yes, respect it. But do not buy into the fear. The spirits do not care about your labels. The Cunning Witch's authority comes from results, not a certificate. My mixed heritage—a blend of cultures often suppressed or ignored—gives me the right to share this. I have lived on the edge of acceptance my entire life, and that friction is where real power is forged.

Light, Dark, and The Grey
You will find people who scream "Love and Light" while judging you for owning a Tarot deck. I had a Christian friend once who was fine with my clairvoyance—attributing it to angels—but was terrified of Tarot cards because they were "evil." The irony is that she was fine with me working with "spirits" as long as they fit her narrative. But tools like Tarot or Ouija are just that: tools. They can open doors to the divine, or they can invite in a world of pain if you don't know what you are doing.

I am not a "love and light" person, but I come from a good place. All my clients know they are my priority and that I am there to help them. But, I deal in the polar opposite. If you are outside my fold and see my kindness as weakness, remember one thing:
If you fuck with me, or the people I love, you will always get the polar opposite.
You won't find a boring history textbook here.
I am here to give you the spells—the tools to protect, defend, and survive.

Welcome to the dark.

Spells Chapter 1: Protection

Protective Magick

Protection
The First Rule of Power

Before you cast a single hex, command a demon, or draw down prosperity, you must understand this fundamental truth: Your protection is non-negotiable.

A powerful witch is not protected by luck; they are protected by layers of meticulously cast intent and wards. Without proper defense, your own power, or the backlash from the entities you command, will crush you. Do not be careless.

1. The Obsidian Mirror Box (Reflecting the Attack)

This is your primary, heavy-duty ward against curses, hexes, and psychic attacks. It doesn't just block; it returns the attack to the sender, amplified.

TOOLS:
- A small wooden or cardboard box with a lid.
- Obsidian Shard or large Black Tourmaline piece (the return conductor).
- Black Salt (to absorb and transmute energy).
- A small mirror that fits inside the box.

METHOD:
1. Prep the Box: Cleanse the box with smoke. Line the inside base of the box with the mirror, facing upwards (reflecting the interior).
2. The Charge: Place the Obsidian/Tourmaline on top of the mirror. Fill the surrounding area with Black Salt.
3. The Command: Seal the box with tape or melted black wax. As you seal it, hold it tightly and command: "My defense is absolute. All malice sent my way is absorbed by this dark stone, magnified by this glass, and instantly returned to the fool who sent it. This box seals my peace. I am safe. I am guarded. It is done."
4. Placement: Place the box above a door, in a secluded corner of your bedroom, or anywhere high up. Never open it. Recharge it with focused intent once a month.

Protection
The First Rule of Power

2. The Black Candle Ward (Active Defence)

Use this as a quick, active defense when you feel an attack is currently in progress.

TOOLS:
- One Black Taper Candle (absorbs negative energy).
- Protective Oil (e.g., Rosemary, Rue, or any protective oil).
- A pinch of Red Pepper Flakes (to give the defense a kick).

METHOD:
1. **Dress the Candle:** Dress the candle from wick to base with the oil (pulling energy to the candle for absorption). Roll the candle in the pepper flakes.
2. **The Burn:** Light the candle and focus on the flame consuming the attack. Command the fire to stand as an impassable barrier between you and the sender.
3. **The Command:** "Fire burns the boundary. You cannot touch me. I am shielded by my will. This flame consumes all malice and returns it as a debt. I am protected, now and always. So mote it be."
4. **Disposal:** Allow the candle to burn down completely. Dispose of the wax remnants off your property.

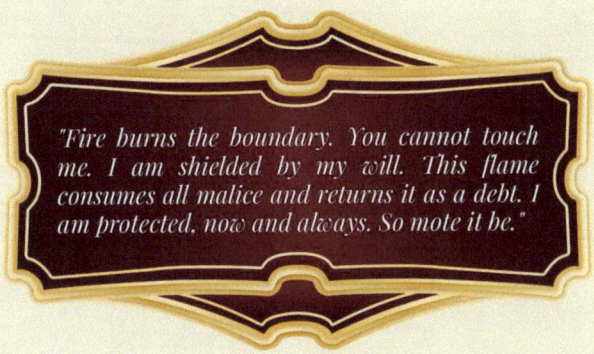

"Fire burns the boundary. You cannot touch me. I am shielded by my will. This flame consumes all malice and returns it as a debt. I am protected, now and always. So mote it be."

Spells Chapter 2: Manifestation

Attraction & Wealth

Manifestation
Attraction and Wealth

"Money flows to me constantly. Every doo[r of] opportunity is mine. I [am a magnet for] wealth, luxury, and ab[undance. I demand] this prosperity. It is don[e."]

Protection secures your foundation; manifestation builds your empire. This is the magick of demand, not desire. You do not wait for the universe to decide you are worthy; you command the universe to deliver the wealth, opportunities, and success you claim as yours.

1. The High-Roller Abundance Jar

This is a continuous working designed to ensure money constantly flows to you from expected and unexpected sources.

TOOLS:
- A jar with a tight lid.
- Cinnamon sticks and Bay Leaves (for speed and wishes).
- High-value currency (a dollar bill, a $20 bill, or a foreign bill—must be real currency).
- Pyrite or Citrine stone (attraction magnets).
- Gold glitter or flakes (to attract luxury).
- Sweetener (Honey or Brown Sugar—to make the money flow sweetly to you).

METHOD:
1. **Cleanse the Money:** Cleanse the currency by passing it through smoke (sage or sweetgrass). Fold it toward you three times, stating: "Come to me and multiply."
2. **The Assembly:** Place the folded money and the stones into the jar. Layer the cinnamon, bay leaves, glitter, and fill the jar with honey/sugar.
3. **The Command:** Seal the jar tightly. Shake it while visualizing a bank account statement with a number so large it makes you smile. Command: "Money flows to me now, easily and constantly. Every door is open, every opportunity is mine. I am a magnet for wealth, luxury, and abundance. I demand this prosperity. It is done."
4. **Placement:** Place the jar near your front door, in your office, or on a high shelf in a beautiful spot. You must treat it like a valuable, sacred object.

Manifestation
Attraction and Wealth

2. The Success and Victory Wash

A ritual wash used before high-stakes events (job interviews, negotiations, court appearances) to ensure you walk in radiating dominance and confidence.

TOOLS:
- Water.
- Cinnamon (speed and victory).
- Five-Finger Grass (to grab and hold success).
- A few drops of your best perfume/cologne (to magnetize your energy).

METHOD:
1. **The Mix:** Warm the water slightly. Add the cinnamon and five-finger grass. Let it steep until the mixture smells potent.
2. **The Command:** Hold the bowl and state: "This water grants me victory. This wash wraps me in undeniable success. I am confident, I am magnetic, and I am the winner of this day. All eyes see my power."
3. **The Wash:** Use the mixture to wash your hands, face, and neck before the event. Do not dry completely; allow the water to air dry on your skin to seal the manifestation.

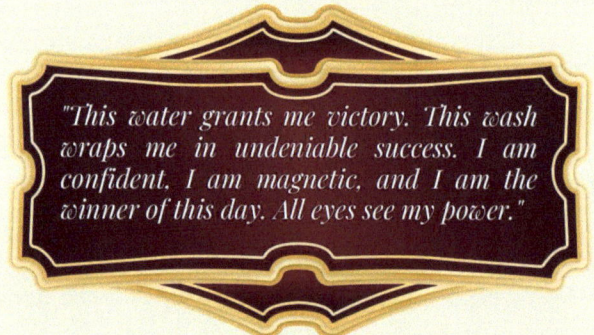

"This water grants me victory. This wash wraps me in undeniable success. I am confident, I am magnetic, and I am the winner of this day. All eyes see my power."

Spells Chapter 3: Where to Start

Mindset & Preparation

Where to Start
Mindset & Preparation

You have secured your defense and commanded your attraction. Now, before you launch into the heavy artillery—the banishing, the domination, the curses—you must check your footing. Magick demands clarity. A messy mind equals messy results.

1. The Mindset Check (Your Absolute Truth)

Stop the spell before it starts if you are feeling desperate, guilty, or uncertain. Your magick flows from your absolute will, not your need.

- **Ask Yourself:** Is this command justified by my truth? Does the debt warrant the severity of the action? If the answer is yes, proceed without apology.
- **Release the Outcome:** Do the work, state the command, and then release the result. Obsession blocks the flow. The Cunning Witch trusts her power and moves on.

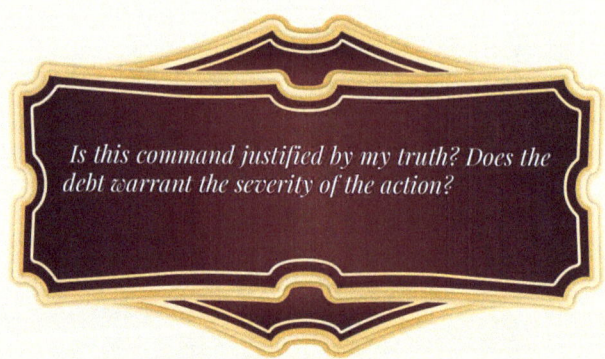

Is this command justified by my truth? Does the debt warrant the severity of the action?

Where to Start
Mindset & Preparation

2. The Clean Slate Clarity Wash

This is a preparatory cleansing ritual used right before starting any major spell (especially those involving banishing or cursing) to clear your head and ensure your intention is pure, unpolluted will.

TOOLS:
- A basin of warm water.
- A few drops of Eucalyptus or Peppermint essential oil (for mental sharpness).
- A pinch of Black Salt (to absorb lingering doubt or fear).
- A small White or Purple candle.

METHOD:
1. **The Mix:** Light the candle for clarity. Add the oils and Black Salt to the warm water, stirring clockwise (to bring things in).
2. **The Command:** Hold the basin and look at your reflection in the water. Command: "My mind is clear, my will is sharp. I see my target and my purpose without distortion. All confusion, fear, and doubt are absorbed by the salt and expelled from my being. I am pure intent."
3. **The Wash:** Wash your hands, face, and the back of your neck with the water. As you do, visualize a heavy cloak of noise and doubt falling off you.
4. **Disposal:** Pour the water down the sink immediately, stating: "Gone and never to return."

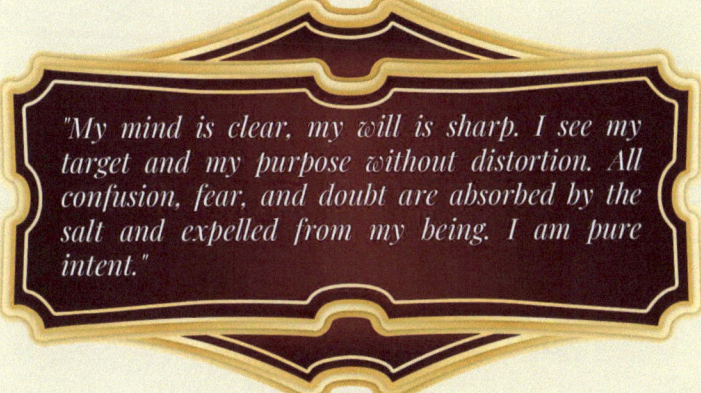

"My mind is clear, my will is sharp. I see my target and my purpose without distortion. All confusion, fear, and doubt are absorbed by the salt and expelled from my being. I am pure intent."

Where to Start
Mindset & Preparation

3. The Power of the Physical Seal (Sealing the Intent)
A spell is not finished until it is physically sealed. This step is non-negotiable and provides the final physical anchor for your non-physical command.

METHOD:
- **The Seal:** Use wax from a sealing candle (black for hexing, white for protection, purple for domination) to drip over the object (jar lid, paper, knot). This physically locks the intent into the object.
- **The Activation:** Once the wax hardens, lightly touch it and state your final command: "Sealed by fire, bound by earth. The work is done. So it is."

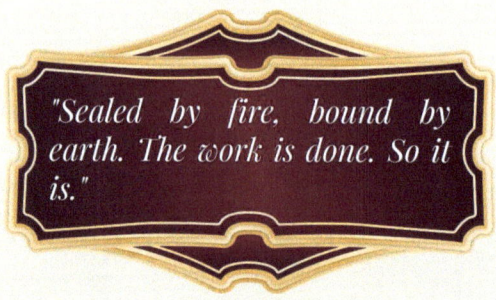

Spells Chapter 4: Dominance

& Influence

Dominance & Influence

This is the control center. Domination spells are essential for the Cunning Witch because they allow you to influence the outcomes of meetings, court cases, arguments, and business deals. This is about making people see things your way and ensuring your authority is respected.

1. The Command Candle Spell
A fast-acting, highly focused spell for influencing a specific person or decision.

TOOLS:
- A purple or blue taper candle (Purple for power/influence, Blue for communication/truth).
- Command or Domination Oil (or a mix of Cinnamon, Bay Leaf, and a bit of whiskey).
- A carving tool.
- A piece of paper and a pen.

METHOD:
1. Carve the Command: Carve the target's name from wick to base (to push your will into them). On the opposite side, carve your specific command (e.g., "Name agrees with my proposal," "Name is silent in court," "Name respects my decision.")
2. Dress the Candle: Anoint the candle with the domination oil, drawing the oil from the top down to the bottom, pushing your will onto the candle.
3. Write the Outcome: On the paper, write a detailed description of the outcome as if it has already happened. Example: "I am thrilled that [Name] signed the contract today and agreed to all my terms. It was an easy, unanimous decision."
4. Burn it Down: Place the candle on top of the folded paper. Light the candle and focus your will on the flame.

THE COMMAND (Speak 3 Times with Authority):
"I am the will, and you are the way. Your mind is bent, your resistance lost. You will submit to my truth, and you will agree to my terms. My word is law. It is done."

1. Let it Manifest: Let the candle burn all the way down. Keep the paper and the remaining wax until the desired outcome manifests, then dispose of it.

Dominance
& Influence

2. The Shut Up & Agree Wash (Mouth-Closing)

Use this when you need someone to stop gossiping, stop arguing with you, or simply agree with your statements.

TOOLS:
1. Cold water.
2. Alum powder (used for pickling, creates a puckering, tongue-drying effect).
3. A few drops of Domination Oil.

METHOD:
1. The Mix: Mix the alum powder into the cold water until it dissolves. Add the domination oil.
2. The Command: Hold the water and command it: "This water silences all dissent. This water binds the tongue. [Name] cannot speak against me, nor argue with my word. They accept my truth. They are silent and compliant."
3. The Application: Use this water to wipe down the handle of a doorknob they use, the edge of a chair they sit on, or lightly mist the air in their direction.
4. If Self-Applied: If you need to dominate a conversation (e.g., before a tough meeting), lightly mist your tongue with the water or wipe a small amount on your lips. This ensures your words are commanding and theirs are reduced.

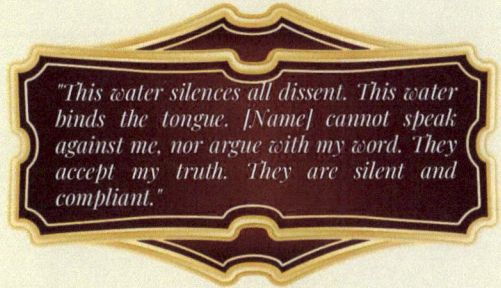

"This water silences all dissent. This water binds the tongue. [Name] cannot speak against me, nor argue with my word. They accept my truth. They are silent and compliant."

Spells Chapter 5: Curses and Hexes

Defence Magick

Defence:
Return to Senders (reversal)

This is the spiritual term for Reversal Magick. If someone sends you fire, you do not block it—you seize it and send back an inferno. This section contains aggressive defensive spells that immediately bounce back and amplify any attack, curse, hex, or psychic drain sent your way. The objective is simple: teach the sender a painful lesson.

1. The Mirror Box Reversal

This is a specific, targeted working designed to catch and instantly return a recognized attack. This differs from the Protection mirror box because it is an active, temporary spell for a single target.

TOOLS:
- A small, sturdy box.
- A shard of broken mirror (to shatter their intent).
- The name of the sender written on paper (if known) or a representation of their energy.
- Black Salt (to absorb the lingering residue of the attack).
- Black candle wax (for sealing).

METHOD:
1. Prep the Mirror: Write the sender's name on the back of the mirror shard. If you don't know the name, simply write "The Sender of Harm."
2. The Assembly: Place the mirror shard, reflective side facing up, inside the box. Place the name paper on the mirror. Sprinkle heavily with Black Salt.
3. The Command: Seal the box with the lid and then with black wax. Command:
4. "What you send is reflected. What you sent is shattered. I do not claim this curse, and I send it back, threefold and swift. May you feel the full weight of the malice you cast. You are the victim of your own will. It is done."
5. Disposal: The moment you feel the energy shift and the curse lift, bury the box off your property (to ground the residual energy) or drop it at a crossroads (to send the energy far away).

Defence:
Return to Senders (reversal)

2. The Reversal Candle Spell

A highly visual and dramatic spell for actively burning off a curse and sending the residual energy back.

TOOLS:
1. One Black Taper Candle (to absorb the negative energy).
2. One White Taper Candle (to represent your clarity and protection).
3. Reversal or Van Van Oil (or a blend of Rosemary and Cayenne Pepper).
4. String or yarn.

METHOD:
1. The Connection: Tie the black and white candles together with the string. Ensure they are close, but the wicks are separated.
2. The Dress: Dress the black candle from top to bottom (pulling the curse into it). Dress the white candle from bottom to top (raising your protection).
3. The Burn: Light the black candle first, then the white candle immediately after. As the black candle burns down, it consumes the curse, while the white candle's flame burns higher, pushing the dark energy away.
4. The Command: Focus on the candles burning the string and the connection dissolving. Command: "The black absorbs the filth; the white returns the debt. The cord is cut. The attack is seized. Go back, go back, go back to the source from which you came. You are disarmed. I am free. It is done."
5. Disposal: The moment the string snaps and the candles are separated by fire, you know the connection is broken. Let the candles burn down completely and dispose of the black candle's wax far away from your home.

Spells Chapter 6: Banishing

Getting Rid of Someone

Banishing:
Getting Rid of Someone

This chapter is for when you need a swift, permanent separation. Banishing is not about subtle suggestion; it is a command for removal. These spells are designed to make a toxic person's life uncomfortable, forcing them to move, change jobs, or simply exit your sphere of influence entirely.

1. The Freezer Banishing Spell

This is the ultimate separation spell, designed to freeze the person's ability to act against you, speak, or move forward in your life.

TOOLS:
- A plastic container with a tight lid (must be freezer-safe).
- A piece of paper with the target's name written nine times.
- Water.
- Black pepper or Chili Flakes (to create chaos or burning pain for them).
- A few small items of symbolic filth (e.g., dirt from a graveyard, used kitty litter, or dust from under your carpet).
- Vinegar (to sour and spoil their happiness).

METHOD:
1. Write and Curse: Write the target's name and fold the paper away from you three times (to push them away). As you fold, spit or breathe your intent onto the paper.
2. The Assembly: Place the folded paper, pepper/chili flakes, symbolic filth, and vinegar into the container. Fill the rest of the container with water.
3. The Command: Seal the container and shake it violently while visualizing the person becoming confused, agitated, and desperate to leave. Command:
4. "I freeze your path, I freeze your voice, I freeze your malice. You cannot speak my name, you cannot see my face, and you cannot walk my road. Go, leave, vanish, and never return. Be gone from my life now. It is done."
5. Placement: Place the container upside down in the back of your freezer. Do not remove it until the person has completely vanished from your life.

BeWitchy® Copyright © 2026 by Madame Verveine / The Devil's Crypt Pty Ltd / BeWitchy. All Rights Reserved.

Banishing:
Getting Rid of Someone

2. Go Away & Stay Away Road Opener
A spell focused on not just removing them, but ensuring their path leads far away from yours.

TOOLS:
- A handful of Gravel or Dirt from a dusty road or intersection.
- A piece of paper with the target's name.
- Black Salt.
- A small cloth bag or paper packet.

METHOD:
1. **Write and Fold:** Write the target's name once on the paper and fold it away from you.
2. **The Assembly:** Place the folded name, the road dirt/gravel, and the Black Salt into the cloth bag.
3. **The Command:** Hold the bag and command it to carry the person far away: "Your road is long, and your direction is away from me. I give you the path; now walk it. You are unwelcome here. Go far, go now, and never seek my presence again. So be it."
4. **The Walk:** Walk the bag to a busy intersection or a road that leads away from your property. Throw the bag over your shoulder without looking back, then walk home a different way.

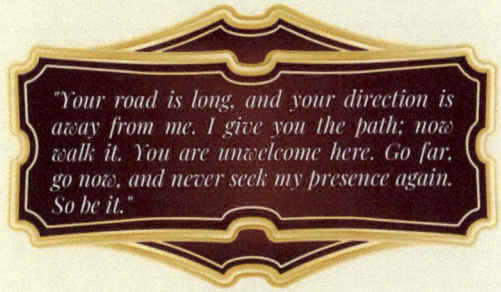

"Your road is long, and your direction is away from me. I give you the path; now walk it. You are unwelcome here. Go far, go now, and never seek my presence again. So be it."

Banishing:
Getting Rid of Someone

3. The Separation Bath (Dissolving Ties)

Use this as a self-cleanse when you feel psychologically or spiritually bound to the person you are banishing, ensuring the emotional cord is severed.

TOOLS:
1. A bath (or basin for a shower).
2. A handful of plain Sea Salt (for cutting ties).
3. A handful of Black Pepper (to repel and irritate the link).
4. A few drops of cutting or uncrossing oil (or Lemon/Lime oil).

METHOD:
1. **The Mix:** Draw your bath and dissolve the salt and pepper into the water. Add the oil.
2. **The Command:** Step into the water and visualize the toxic person's energy as a dark, muddy color clinging to your skin. Command: "I cut all ties of malice and connection. I dissolve your hold on my peace. Your energy washes away now. I am free of your influence. Severed, dissolved, gone."
3. **The Wash:** Submerge yourself fully (if safe) or use a cup to pour the water over your head. As the water drains, visualize their energy running down the drain and leaving your house forever.
4. **Cleanse:** Step out and immediately shower with clean water and soap to fully wash away the residue. Do not dry with a towel; air dry if possible.

Spells Chapter 7: Exorcisms

Cleansing Spiritual Clutter

Exorcisms:
Cleansing Spiritual Clutter

An exorcism in Cunning Magick is not a drama filled with holy water and priests; it is a clinical, powerful command to remove an entity, attachment, or deeply embedded negative energy. You are the final authority in your space. This section ensures your domain remains clean, focused, and purely under your control.

1. The Heavy-Duty Room Purge (Smoke and Sound)

Use this when you feel a heavy, lingering oppression, cold spots, or a general sense of unease or hostility in a space.

TOOLS:
- High-quality Frankincense and Myrrh resin (for raising vibrations and spiritual cleansing).
- Charcoal briquettes (for burning the resin).
- A small drum, chime, or bell (for vibration and sound).
- A commanding tone of voice.

METHOD:
1. Preparation: Open all windows and doors (physical exits are necessary for the entity). Clear the room of clutter and distractions.
2. Smoke and Sound: Light the charcoal and place the resin on top to create heavy, fragrant smoke. Start at the darkest corner of the room, slowly moving clockwise (to invite new energy) or counter-clockwise (to banish, if the energy is heavily negative).
3. The Command: As you move, beat the drum or ring the chime loudly in every corner and near every window. Command the space:
4. "I am the master of this domain. All uninvited energies, entities, and attachments are commanded to leave this space now. I strip you of your power and your claim. Go through this window, go through this door. Do not linger, and do not return. The space is mine. It is cleansed. It is done."
5. Seal and Recharge: Once the smoke clears, immediately light a white candle for peace and protection, and a yellow candle for joy and clarity. Shut the doors.

Exorcisms:
Cleansing Spiritual Clutter

2. The Personal Exorcism Wash (Body and Aura)

Use this when you feel an entity or attachment is specifically clinging to you or affecting your sleep and mood.

TOOLS:
1. A bath (or basin for a shower).
2. High-quality Lemon or Lime Juice (to cut ties and purify).
3. A large handful of Epsom Salts (to draw out deep negativity).
4. Rue or Hyssop herb (for uncrossing and protection).

METHOD:
1. **The Mix:** Draw your bath and dissolve the Epsom salts. Add the lemon/lime juice and the herbs.
2. **The Command:** Submerge yourself fully. Focus on the water as a vibrating blade cutting away invisible cords. Command: "I sever the tie. I cut the cord. All that clings to my aura, to my mind, and to my skin is cut away now. I am whole, I am clean, and I am sealed against all intrusion. I am purified. It is done."
3. **The Wash:** Remain in the water for at least five minutes. As you drain the water, visualize the darkness leaving your body and flowing down the drain.
4. **Grounding:** Immediately dress in clean clothes. Drink a glass of cold water and eat a small piece of food to ground your energy. Do not engage in further magickal work for one hour.

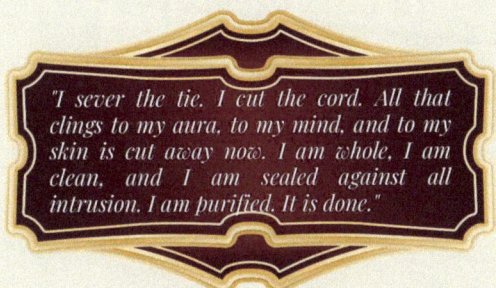

"I sever the tie. I cut the cord. All that clings to my aura, to my mind, and to my skin is cut away now. I am whole, I am clean, and I am sealed against all intrusion. I am purified. It is done."

Spells Chapter 8: Love Spells

Attraction & Influence

Love Spells:
Attraction & Influence

Love in Cunning Magick is not about passive waiting; it is about magnetic attraction and ensuring your desired partner sees only you. These spells are designed for self-empowerment, confidence boosting, and drawing in the energy of someone you desire. Remember, intent is everything: be honest about whether you are attracting love or simply dominating a specific person's free will.

1. The Undeniable Attraction Powder

This is a personal, wearable charm designed to make you irresistible, drawing attention, compliments, and magnetic attraction from all who encounter you, especially your target.

TOOLS:
- Cinnamon (for attraction and heat).
- Rose petals, dried (for love and affection).
- Gold or Pink Glitter (for irresistible sparkle and noticeability).
- A few drops of your signature perfume/cologne.
- A small, clean makeup brush or powder puff.

METHOD:
1. The Mix: Grind the dried rose petals and cinnamon into a fine powder. Mix thoroughly with the gold/pink glitter.
2. The Charge: Place the powder in a clean jar. Add a few drops of your perfume. Close the lid and charge the mix with your intent, visualizing yourself walking into a room and instantly captivating every eye.
3. The Command: Hold the jar and command:
4. "My presence is captivating. My light is irresistible. I draw love, desire, and affection from all I encounter. [Name of Target, if specific] sees only me and desires only my touch. I am magnetism made flesh. It is done."
5. The Application: Use the puff or brush to lightly dust the powder onto your pulse points (neck, wrists) or sweep it lightly over your hair before meeting your target or entering a social space.

Love Spells:
Attraction & Influence

2. The Honey Jar Sweetener (For Communication)

Use this to sweeten a relationship, or to make a specific person's words, thoughts, and feelings toward you overwhelmingly sweet and positive.

TOOLS:
- A small jar with a lid.
- Pure Honey or Brown Sugar.
- A piece of paper with the target's name written nine times.
- Rose quartz shard (for loving energy).

METHOD:
1. The Write: Write the target's name nine times on the paper, crossing each name with your own command (e.g., "Name thinks sweet thoughts about me"). Fold the paper toward you.
2. The Assembly: Place the paper and the rose quartz in the bottom of the jar. Fill the jar completely with honey or pack it tightly with brown sugar.
3. The Command: Seal the jar. Hold it and visualize the honey dissolving any bitterness or resistance. Command:
4. "Your words are sweet, your thoughts are kind, your heart turns toward mine. All friction is dissolved in sweetness. You crave my presence, you speak my praises. Only good things flow between us. Sweetness now binds us. It is done."
5. Placement: Place the jar in a warm, dark place (like a closet or under a bed) to keep the intention constantly "cooking." Give it a gentle shake once a week to stir the energy.

Spells Chapter 9: Curses

Aggressive Magick

Curses: Cursing

Curses and hexes are tools, and the Cunning Witch is a master mechanic. This is not about playground revenge; this is about ensuring justice when the legal or moral world fails you. When you curse, you are deploying a focused, controlled, and painful spiritual attack on someone who has earned your wrath. This requires precision, conviction, and zero remorse.

1. The Sour Jar Curse (Rotting Their Fortune)

This curse is designed to ruin a person's luck, sour their relationships, and spoil their opportunities, creating chaos and bitterness in their life.

TOOLS:
- A jar with a tight lid.
- White Vinegar or Pickle Juice (to sour and spoil).
- A piece of paper with the target's name and date of birth written nine times.
- Thumbtacks, rusty nails, or broken glass shards (to cause pain and chaos).
- Chili Powder or Cayenne Pepper (to bring heat, agitation, and trouble).

METHOD:
1. The Write: Write the target's name nine times on the paper, crossing each name with a specific command (e.g., "Name loses their job," "Name's relationship sours," "Name is agitated and unhappy."). Fold the paper away from you three times.
2. The Assembly: Place the folded paper, the sharp metal, and the chili powder into the jar. Fill the jar completely with vinegar or pickle juice.
3. The Command: Seal the jar tightly. Shake it violently while screaming or hissing the person's name and commanding the chaos you wish upon them.
4. "I spoil your peace, I sour your path, I pierce your happiness. Every day is sharp, every interaction is bitter. Your luck rots. Your joy is spoiled. Feel the fire of your karma now. It is done."
5. Placement: Store the jar in a cold, dark place (like a freezer, if you want to freeze their ability to change the situation, or buried in the earth far from your home to ground the bad energy).

BeWitchy® Copyright © 2026 by Madame Verveine / The Devil's Crypt Pty Ltd / BeWitchy. All Rights Reserved.

Curses:
Cursing

2. The Black Salt Foot Track Curse (Driving Them Away)

A direct and immediate curse designed to cause the target discomfort, unrest, and a compelling need to leave their current space or situation.

TOOLS:
1. Black Salt (your curse carrier).
2. A pinch of Dirt from your property (to ground the curse).
3. Cayenne Pepper or Red Brick Dust (to cause hot feet and restlessness).

METHOD:
1. **The Mix:** Mix the Black Salt, dirt, and Cayenne Pepper thoroughly. Visualize the mix as pure, destructive energy.
2. **The Command:** Hold the mixture and command it: "This salt burns your feet. This dust commands you to wander. You find no rest, you find no peace. Stay only until you must leave. Your feet carry you away from me now. Go, go, go!"
3. **The Application:** Scatter the mixture where the target will physically walk over it. The most effective spots are across their threshold (front door), across their office entrance, or dusted on the floor where they sit.

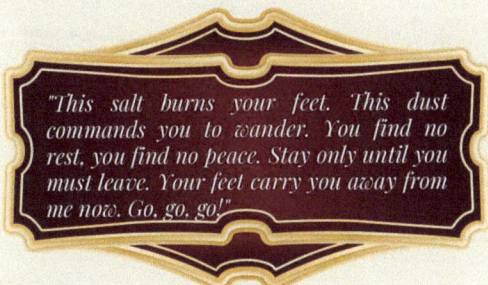

"This salt burns your feet. This dust commands you to wander. You find no rest, you find no peace. Stay only until you must leave. Your feet carry you away from me now. Go, go, go!"

Curses:
Cursing

3. The Candle Wax Figure Hex (Binding and Illness)

A powerful form of sympathetic magick used to cause general ill-health, sluggishness, or binding of the target's will.

TOOLS:
- Black candle wax (melted).
- A small stick or tool for shaping.
- A piece of the target's DNA (hair, nail clipping) or a taglock (their photo/name paper).
- A sewing needle or sharp pin.

METHOD:
1. Shape the Figure: Melt the black wax and quickly shape it into a rough human figure (a poppet). As the wax cools, embed the target's DNA/taglock into the chest area.
2. The Charge: Hold the figure and name it after the target: "You are now [Target's Name]. You answer to me."
3. The Action: Focus on the specific illness or weakness you wish to inflict. Heat the pin/needle and slowly drive it into the corresponding area of the wax figure (e.g., into the head for confusion, into the legs for immobility, into the chest for low energy).
4. The Command: As you insert the pin, command: "I bind your health. I drain your strength. You feel the constant weight of my command. You are weak, you are sluggish, and you cannot succeed. You are bound by my will. It is done."
5. Placement: Wrap the figure in black cloth and keep it in a secure location where it will not be disturbed, ensuring the curse remains active.

Spells Chapter 10: Demon Attack

Forceful Banishing

Demon Attack:
Forceful Banishing

When you are dealing with demonic energies, you are no longer dealing with simple curses or lingering attachments—you are facing entities of pure malice and intent. This requires an immediate, powerful, and commanding response. Your authority is everything. You do not ask; you command it to leave.

1. The Immediate Black Fire Banishing

Use this spell the moment you feel a physical, cold, or intensely hostile presence. This is designed to create a painful barrier that forces the entity to retreat.

TOOLS:
- Black Salt (for creating a barrier).
- A piece of paper with the Demon's name (if known) or "DEMON" written across it.
- A strong, clean alcohol (like Vodka or Whiskey) or Florida Water.
- A commanding voice (fear is a weakness the entity will exploit).

METHOD:
1. The Barrier: Immediately sprinkle a line of Black Salt across the threshold of the door or room where the presence is felt.
2. The Write: Place the name paper on a fire-safe plate or bowl. Pour a small amount of the alcohol/Florida Water over the paper.
3. The Command: Light the paper on fire. As it burns, stomp your foot hard and command the entity using its name (or "DEMON") with absolute authority:
4. "I am the sovereign of this space. I am the will of this domain. You are UNWELCOME and you are COMMANDED to retreat now! Feel the fire of your removal! Go back to the void and never return! The door is sealed, and you are banished. It is done."
5. Seal and Cleanse: Let the paper burn completely. Take the ashes and immediately dispose of them outside, far from your property. Immediately re-cleanse the space with sound or Frankincense smoke.

Demon Attack:
Forceful Banishing

2. The Command to Michael (High-Vibrational Shield)

When dealing with dark entities, sometimes calling on a high-level force of light/justice is the fastest way to get removal. This is not prayer; it is a spiritual contract and deployment of a higher power.

TOOLS:
- One bright Blue Candle (for protection and truth).
- A drop of Frankincense Oil (to raise vibrations).
- A piece of silver jewelry (to act as a temporary focus/anchor).

METHOD:
1. **The Charge:** Light the blue candle. Hold the silver object (or place it on your chest). Focus all your intent on the Archangel Michael (or any high-level protective entity you trust).
2. **The Command:** Speak directly to the entity you are commanding: "Michael, Sword of Justice, I deploy your power now. Stand as a shield against this darkness. Cut the cords, sever the attachment, and remove this unwelcome energy from my presence immediately. You are my sword. Guard my space. It is done."
3. **The Seal:** Let the candle burn for at least one hour while you feel the cleansing energy work. Wear the silver object for the next 24 hours to maintain the shield.

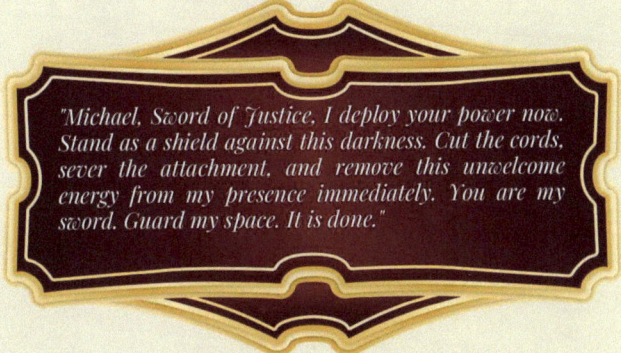

"Michael, Sword of Justice, I deploy your power now. Stand as a shield against this darkness. Cut the cords, sever the attachment, and remove this unwelcome energy from my presence immediately. You are my sword. Guard my space. It is done."

Spells Chapter 11: Death Spells

The Final Command

Death Spells:
The Final Command

In Cunning Magick, "Death" often refers to the death of influence, luck, reputation, or future opportunity for your enemy. These are the spells of absolute finality, used when banishing and cursing have failed, or when the injustice demands a complete spiritual severance. Proceed with absolute conviction and be prepared to accept the consequences of this high-level work.

1. The Deep Freeze & Burial Spell

This spell is designed to stop the target's life in its tracks, burying their ability to succeed, find peace, or move forward in any positive direction.

TOOLS:
- A sturdy, black freezer bag or container.
- A piece of paper with the target's name, date of birth, and a photo (if possible).
- Sour ingredients (rotten food, moldy bread, sour milk/vinegar) to signify decay.
- Grave dirt (collected respectfully, or black dirt from under a dying tree).
- A few small bones or teeth (symbolic of spiritual death).

METHOD:
1. The Write: Write the target's name nine times. Fold the paper away from you three times.
2. The Command: As you fold, breathe your final command of removal and stop onto the paper. State: "Your life is over. Your luck is buried."
3. The Assembly: Place the folded paper, the rotten/sour ingredients, the grave dirt, and the bones into the bag/container. Fill with the sour milk or vinegar to ensure complete spoiling.
4. The Final Seal: Seal the container tightly. Command one last time:
5. "I bury your success. I stop your path. I freeze your influence. Your name will be remembered only in failure and darkness. All good things are dead to you. You are permanently removed from my world. It is finished."
6. Placement: Place the container deep in the back of your freezer, under bags of frozen items, to ensure their life remains stopped. Alternatively, for a literal "burial," bury the container at the foot of an old, dying tree far from your property.

Death Spells:
The Final Command

2. The Vanishing Flame Ritual

A ritual focused on dissolving the target's existence and presence in the world, ensuring they fade from memory and relevance.

TOOLS:
- A small black bowl or fire-safe dish.
- A piece of paper with the target's name (written faintly).
- Dried Mugwort (for dissolving and invisibility).
- Sulphur powder or Match Heads (for swift, powerful burning).
- A commanding oil (Domination or Cursing oil).

METHOD:
1. Prep the Paper: Lightly rub the name paper with the commanding oil. Sprinkle the Mugwort and Sulphur/Match Heads over the paper.
2. The Burn: Light the paper on fire using a black candle. Watch the paper burn completely, visualizing the target's image, voice, and name turning to dust and smoke.
3. The Command: As the flame consumes the paper, command: "Your presence vanishes. Your memory fades. You are forgotten by those who matter. Your future is ash. You have no relevance, no voice, and no power here. You are dissolved and gone. Let the smoke carry your essence away."
4. Disposal: Gather the ashes and immediately dispose of them into running water (a stream or toilet) to carry the essence away, ensuring they can never return or reform.

Spells Chapter 12: Funny Spells

Petty & Effective Magick

Funny Spells:
Petty & Effective Magick

Not every problem requires a full-scale curse or a demonic banishment. Sometimes, a person just needs a little, continuous annoyance until they get the hint. This chapter is for the petty, low-stakes magick that solves minor issues quickly and often provides you with a much-needed laugh. Use with zero guilt.

1. The Perpetual Itch & Annoyance Jar

This spell is designed to make the target continuously uncomfortable, agitated, and itchy in their current situation (job, relationship, home) until they are forced to leave or change.

TOOLS:
- A jar with a lid.
- A piece of paper with the target's name.
- Black Pepper (for agitation and irritation).
- Sandpaper or a rough stone (to represent the constant itching/friction).
- A few drops of any sour liquid (vinegar, lemon juice).
- A strong elastic band or rubber band.

METHOD:
1. The Write: Write the target's name and the specific annoyance (e.g., "Name feels agitated and itchy"). Fold the paper away from you.
2. The Assembly: Place the paper, pepper, sandpaper/stone, and sour liquid into the jar. Wrap the rubber band around the jar nine times, snapping it lightly each time to create a sharp, irritating sound.
3. The Command: Seal the jar. Shake it vigorously while visualizing the target scratching, squirming, and being generally miserable until they move on. Command:
4. "Agitation now clings to your skin. Itchiness now lives in your mind. You will find no peace, no comfort, and no rest in this space. Your only relief is distance from me. Go, squirm, and leave. It is done."
5. Placement: Store the jar somewhere you can give it a vigorous shake whenever you think of the target, reinforcing their discomfort.

Funny Spells:
Petty & Effective Magick

2. The Shut Up & Stop Gossiping Powder

A gentle but firm spell to bind the tongue of a gossip or a rude neighbor who won't stop talking about your business.

TOOLS:
- Powdered Sugar (to sweeten their mouth only when they talk about nice things).
- Dried Mint or Gum (to keep their mouth busy).
- Alum Powder (to dry out and constrict the tongue when they speak malice).
- A small piece of paper.

METHOD:
1. The Mix: Mix the sugar, mint, and alum powder.
2. The Command: Hold the mix and command it to control their words: "If you speak my name with kindness, your mouth is sweet. If you speak malice, your tongue shall cleave. Gossip stops now. You are silent about my affairs. Only kind words remain."
3. The Application: Write the target's name on the paper and fold it away from you. Sprinkle a small amount of the powder onto the folded paper. Place the paper and powder near where the gossip lives (by their window, under their mailbox, or dusted on their doorknob).
4. Disposal: The rest of the powder can be stored and used as needed until the gossip stops.

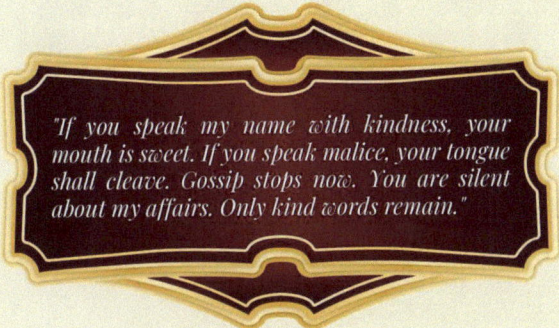

"If you speak my name with kindness, your mouth is sweet. If you speak malice, your tongue shall cleave. Gossip stops now. You are silent about my affairs. Only kind words remain."

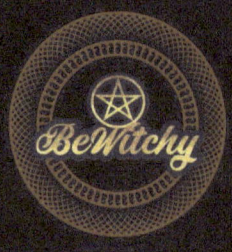

Spells Chapter 13: The Other Spells

A Mix of Black Magick Spells

The Rest
Advanced Recipes

This appendix provides a structured collection of the 43 specialized spells from the complete Cunning Magick Compendium. These recipes are focused on Aggression, Domination, and Self-Service, giving you powerful, detailed instructions for seizing control of any situation.

SECTION A: AGGRESSIVE DEFENSE AND COUNTER-COMMAND (5 Spells)

24. The Crossroads Ward
TOOLS: Gravel from four different roads, a small Black Tourmaline stone, Red Brick Dust.

METHOD:
1. Mix the gravel, Black Tourmaline, and Red Brick Dust together. Visualize this mix as a highly confusing, painful spiritual deterrent.
2. Walk the perimeter of your property, scattering the mix at the edge of your boundaries, or specifically across the entryway.
3. Visualize anyone intending harm becoming hopelessly lost or turned away.

COMMAND (Speak with finality):
"You seek my home, but you find four roads. You seek my peace, but you find confusion. Turn back now. You are disoriented, unwelcome, and cannot locate my domain. It is done."

25. The Four-Corner Barrier
TOOLS: Black Salt, four Iron Nails, Protective Oil (or Clove/Rosemary).

METHOD:
1. Dress the four iron nails with the Protective Oil, visualizing them as sharp, impenetrable stakes.
2. Walk to each of the four outermost corners of your property.
3. Hammer one nail into the ground at each corner, then sprinkle Black Salt over the spot where the nail entered the earth.

COMMAND (Spoken at each corner):
"I pin this barrier down. The walls are sealed, the boundary is firm, and all harm is repelled by this iron will. This space is protected. Nothing unwanted enters. It is done."

The Rest
Advanced Recipes

26. Garlic Knot Bind

TOOLS: Three fresh garlic cloves (for venom), Red Thread (for binding).

METHOD:
1. Hold the three garlic cloves and name them after the three biggest pieces of gossip or lies being told about you.
2. Using the red thread, tightly wrap the three cloves together, binding them into a tight knot.
3. Say your command as you tie the final, tightest knot. Dispose of the knot by burying it deep off your property.

COMMAND (Spoken while binding):
"I tie the tongue. I bind the venom. This gossip is tied, sealed, and silent. Your words are stuck, your mouth is bound. Speak no more of me. It is done."

27. House Shield Dust

TOOLS: Powdered eggshell (for cleansing/barrier), Sage ash (for purity), Cumin (for fidelity/protection).

METHOD:
1. Mix the powdered eggshell, sage ash, and cumin into a fine dust.
2. Stand at your main door (inside). Take a pinch of the dust and blow it outwards across the threshold, covering the frame and sill.
3. Renew as needed, especially after visitors leave.

COMMAND (Spoken as you blow the dust):
"This shield is invisible and strong. Only peace and prosperity shall pass this line. All malice, ill will, and intrusive energy are rejected now. This home is sealed. It is done."

The Rest
Advanced Recipes

28. Astral Net Trap

TOOLS: A White Quartz stone (for clarity), Lavender (for sleep/peace), Small Mesh Bag.

METHOD:
1. Place the White Quartz and Lavender buds inside the mesh bag.
2. Hold the bag and command it to guard your subconscious while you sleep.
3. Place the bag directly under your pillow or mattress before going to bed.

COMMAND (Whispered):
"While my body rests, my spirit is safe. This net catches all ill will, all psychic theft, and all harmful dreams. My sleep is sacred, my mind is sealed. I am protected until morning light. It is done."

The Rest
Advanced Recipes

SECTION B: SEIZURE OF FORTUNE AND DOMINATION OF INFLUENCE (10 Spells)

29. Job Stealer Sigil
TOOLS: Green ink, a Bay Leaf (for victory), High John the Conqueror Root (for domination).

METHOD:
1. Using the green ink, draw a sigil representing the specific job title or company success you want on the Bay Leaf.
2. Anoint the Bay Leaf and the High John Root with Success Oil (or Cinnamon).
3. Carry the leaf and root in your pocket to the interview or meeting where the decision is being made. Burn the leaf when you receive the offer.

COMMAND (Spoken before the interview):
"The ground is mine, the victory is sealed. The opportunity seeks me, the competition yields. This job, this title, this power is mine. Command it be so. It is done."

30. Quick Cash Bowl
TOOLS: Seven Coins (current currency), Cinnamon, Green Candle.

METHOD:
1. Place the seven coins in a small bowl. Sprinkle them heavily with Cinnamon (for speed and heat).
2. Place the green candle in the middle of the coins (or beside the bowl).
3. Light the candle and visualize money arriving from unexpected sources (a forgotten check, a sudden bonus, an old debt repaid).

COMMAND (Spoken with urgency):
"Money, come quickly. Cash, come now. I demand seven-fold return and instant flow. This need is met, this bowl is full. Send the resources now. It is done."
 incoming evil eye or negative energy.

The Rest
Advanced Recipes

31. Business Command Lamp
TOOLS: Olive Oil, Basil, Written Petition for growth, Floating wick.

METHOD:
1. Write your business goals or a list of perfect clients on the petition paper. Place it under a glass container.
2. Fill the container with Olive Oil and add dried Basil (for money/business).
3. Place the floating wick in the oil and light it. Let it burn every day for a short period.

COMMAND (Spoken as you light the wick):
"This flame commands attention. This light draws all profitable eyes to my work. My business is active, attractive, and constantly growing. Success is inevitable. It is done."

32. Debt Vanisher Pot
TOOLS: Salt, Water, Written list of debts, Freezer.

METHOD:
1. Write a detailed list of all the debts you wish to dissolve. Fold the paper away from you three times.
2. Place the paper in a container and cover it with water. Add a generous amount of salt (to preserve the "frozen" state).
3. Place the pot in the freezer and forget about it.

COMMAND (Spoken while placing the container in the freezer):
"I stop this flow of debt. I freeze its power, I bind its claim. These obligations are dissolved and cannot touch my funds. Debt vanishes now. It is done."

The Rest
Advanced Recipes

33. Wealth Magnet Wash
TOOLS: Chamomile tea (for luck), Mint leaves (for money), a few drops of Honey (to draw sweetness).

METHOD:
1. Brew the chamomile tea and let it cool. Add the mint leaves and honey.
2. Before going out to handle money, sign documents, or start work, use the mix to wash your hands, visualizing wealth sticking to your fingers.
3. Air dry your hands.

COMMAND (Spoken while washing):
"My hands are magnets for gold. All financial transactions turn to profit. I attract wealth and repel scarcity. My touch is golden. It is done."

34. Client Attractor Box
TOOLS: Dried Orange Peels (for drawing success), a small Magnet, a copy of your Business Card.

METHOD:
1. Place the orange peels (or a small piece of citrus fruit) and your business card inside a small box.
2. Add the magnet, commanding it to pull in perfect clients who pay well.
3. Keep the box near your workspace or cash register.

COMMAND (Spoken over the box):
"Clients crave my work. Prosperity flows to my door. I attract the best, the most profitable, and the most dedicated. Come now, be drawn to my service. It is done."

The Rest
Advanced Recipes

35. Green Salt Circle
TOOLS: Green Salt (dyed with food coloring or herbs), Dried Cloves, Pyrite (Fool's Gold).

METHOD:
1. Mix the Green Salt and Dried Cloves (for luck/money).
2. Create a small circle of this mix around your wallet, a pile of money, or a financial document.
3. Place the Pyrite stone inside the circle overnight to charge the intention.

COMMAND (Spoken over the circle):
"This circle contains continuous gain. Money flows freely and safely within my boundary. I am saturated in green energy. Abundance is my constant state. It is done."

36. Opportunity Road Opener
TOOLS: A Key (symbolic of unlocking), a Cinnamon Stick (for fast success), Olive Oil.

METHOD:
1. Anoint the key and the cinnamon stick with Olive Oil.
2. Hold them together and focus on the specific door or path you need opened (e.g., a promotion, a new venture).
3. Carry the key and stick until the opportunity manifests.

COMMAND (Spoken firmly):
"The path is clear, the door is open. All blockages are removed. Success is swift, and opportunity greets me now. I walk toward victory. It is done."

The Rest
Advanced Recipes

37. Golden Mirror Spell
TOOLS: Small Gold-painted mirror, a significant piece of currency (e.g., $50 note).

METHOD:
1. Tape the currency face-up onto the gold-painted mirror, ensuring the dollar amount is reflected.
2. Place the mirror in a prominent location where you will see it often, reflecting the abundance.
3. Every time you pass the mirror, affirm the influx of wealth.

COMMAND (Spoken directly to the mirror):
"I multiply my resources. I reflect and amplify all incoming wealth. My funds are doubled and protected. My prosperity is infinite. It is done."

38. Prosperity Pocket Charm
TOOLS: Allspice, Basil, Small drawstring bag (green or gold).

METHOD:
1. Mix the Allspice (for luck/speed) and Basil (for wealth) in your hands.
2. Place the mixture into the drawstring bag.
3. Charge the bag by holding it and commanding it to draw money. Carry it in your pocket or wallet at all times.

COMMAND (Spoken over the bag):
"This bag is a constant source of gain. I repel scarcity and attract fortune. I am always in profit. Prosperity travels with me. It is done."

The Rest
Advanced Recipes

SECTION C: EXTREME DOMINATION AND AUTHORITY (5 Spells)

39. Bind the Tongue Hex
TOOLS: Alum powder (to constrict), paper with name, Black thread.

METHOD:
1. Write the target's name on the paper and fold it away from you.
2. Sprinkle alum powder over the folded paper.
3. Wrap the paper tightly with black thread, visualizing their mouth sealed shut regarding your affairs. Bury the packet.

COMMAND (Spoken while binding):
"I bind your malice, I bind your words. Your tongue is dried, your speech is stopped. You cannot speak against me or about my life. You are silenced forever. It is done."

40. Shoe Track Dominance
TOOLS: Dirt from your path (where you walk often), name on paper, Red Wax.

METHOD:
1. Write the target's name on the paper. Place it in a small dish.
2. Sprinkle the dirt from your path over the name.
3. Melt the red wax and pour it over the dirt and paper, sealing the target under your 'road' or path.

COMMAND (Spoken as the wax cools):
"My path is your destination. My will is your command. You walk where I lead, you follow where I step. You are sealed beneath my influence. It is done."

The Rest
Advanced Recipes

41. Mind Control Incense
TOOLS: Lavender, Patchouli, Sandalwood (burnable).

METHOD:
1. Mix the herbs/incense and light them before a meeting or confrontation with the target.
2. As the smoke rises, visualize the target's mind softening, becoming pliable, and accepting your suggestions easily.
3. Carry the scent on your clothing or hair before engaging with the target.

COMMAND (Spoken over the smoke):
"Your mind is open, your resistance is weak. You accept my truth, you agree with my terms. Your judgment is mine to control. Submit now. It is done."

42. The Puppet Hand Charm
TOOLS: Small wooden doll hand or figure, Domination Oil.

METHOD:
1. Dress the doll hand heavily with Domination Oil.
2. Name the hand after the target or the situation you need to control (e.g., "The Board's Decision").
3. Carry the charm in your pocket during the event, squeezing it gently to manipulate the outcome to your desire.

COMMAND (Spoken while charging the hand):
"I hold the strings, I guide the action. The outcome is molded by my will and my touch. You move as I command. The victory is mine. It is done."

The Rest
Advanced Recipes

43. The Follow Command

TOOLS: Sweetener (sugar), Salt (for binding), Target's footprint soil (if possible) or a taglock.

METHOD:
1. Mix the sugar and salt together, visualizing the target being sweetened toward you but bound by the salt.
2. Place the target's soil/taglock into the mix.
3. Sprinkle the mix near their doorway or their car tires, ensuring they physically travel under the spell's influence.

COMMAND (Spoken while sprinkling):
"You are sweet to me, but you are commanded to follow. Your road leads to my door, your loyalty rests with me. Go, but return only to me. It is done."

The Rest
Advanced Recipes

SECTION D: JUSTICE, COURT CASES, AND LEGAL SUBVERSION (4 Spells)

44. Judge's Favour Spell
TOOLS: Blue candle, Dove's Blood Ink (or red ink), Piece of paper shaped like a gavel.

METHOD:
1. Using the ink, write the judge's name and the words "RULES IN MY FAVOR" on the paper gavel.
2. Anoint the blue candle toward you and burn it while visualizing the judge agreeing with your every point.
3. Carry the paper gavel with you to court.

COMMAND (Spoken while burning):
"The scales of justice tip for me. The gavel strikes down only my opponents. The court sees the truth I present. Judge [Name] favors me and rules in my victory. It is done."

45. Confuson in Court
TOOLS: Black pepper, Lemon peel (for sourness/confusion), Name of opposing counsel or witness on paper.

METHOD:
1. Write the names of those you wish to confuse on the paper. Fold it away from you.
2. Mix the black pepper and lemon peel together, grinding them fiercely.
3. Sprinkle the mix on the steps or near the entrance of the courthouse before the trial begins.

COMMAND (Spoken over the powder):
"Chaos reigns in your mind. Your words are mixed, your memory fails, your arguments collapse. You speak only confusion and error. Truth is lost to you. It is done."

The Rest
Advanced Recipes

46. The Truth Binding
TOOLS: Blue thread, White paper, Name of Liar.

METHOD:
1. Write the liar's name on the white paper.
2. Fold the paper toward you (to pull the truth out) and tie it tightly with the blue thread.
3. Suspend the tied paper over a bowl of water or a candle while commanding the truth to be released.

COMMAND (Spoken over the binding):
"The lie is bound, the truth is forced. Your words are clear, your secrets revealed. You cannot hide the reality of this situation. Speak the truth, and nothing less. It is done."

47. Swift Justice Powder
TOOLS: Red Brick Dust (for power/speed), Chili flakes (for heat/urgency), Salt.

METHOD:
1. Mix the Red Brick Dust, Chili flakes, and salt into a powerful powder.
2. Take a small amount and dust it lightly over any court papers, legal notices, or petitions filed in your favor.
3. Focus on the process moving at lightning speed toward your desired verdict.

COMMAND (Spoken over the documents):
"I demand speed, I demand victory, I demand justice now. Move swiftly, move decisively, move toward my success. The verdict is mine. It is done."

The Rest
Advanced Recipes

SECTION E: PERMANENT BANISHING AND REMOVAL (4 Spells)

48. Get Out of My House Wash
TOOLS: Ammonia, Vinegar, Black Salt.

METHOD:
1. Mix equal parts Ammonia and Vinegar (do not inhale). Add a heavy handful of Black Salt.
2. Use this mixture to scrub the floors, windowsills, and door handles, starting at the back of the house and moving towards the front door.
3. Dump the remaining wash outside your house and away from your property.

COMMAND (Spoken while scrubbing):
"This home is cleansed. All uninvited guests, tenants, and unwelcome spirits are commanded to leave. This wash burns your desire to stay. Go now and do not return. It is done."

49. Fast Exit Road Opener
TOOLS: Gravel, Salt, a pair of old Keys.

METHOD:
1. Place the gravel (to provide a road), the salt (to bind the leaving), and the old keys (to unlock the exit) into a pouch.
2. Walk to a crossroads or a road that leads away from your home.
3. Throw the pouch over your shoulder, commanding the person to follow the open road, then walk home a different way.

COMMAND (Spoken as you throw the pouch):
"The road is open, the path is clear. Go far away from me, and travel quickly. The keys unlock your permanent exit. Leave now, and find another place to rest. It is done."

The Rest
Advanced Recipes

50. Mirror Scrying Banishing
TOOLS: Small mirror, Black ink, Burning Banishing Incense (or Sage/Rue).

METHOD:
1. Write the target's name on the mirror in black ink.
2. Burn the Banishing Incense. Look into the mirror through the smoke and visualize the target looking back, seeing a hateful, miserable version of themselves.
3. Command them to leave based on what they see. Wash the name off immediately.

COMMAND (Spoken to the reflection):
"Look upon yourself. Your presence here brings you only misery and pain. Stay and suffer, or leave now and find peace elsewhere. The choice is yours. Go! It is done."

51. The Cold Shoulder Charm
TOOLS: Ice cubes, Lemon juice, Photo of Target (or name on paper).

METHOD:
1. Place the photo/name paper into a small container.
2. Squeeze lemon juice over the paper (to sour the connection).
3. Fill the rest of the container with water and freeze it, commanding all warmth and connection to stop.

COMMAND (Spoken while placing the container in the freezer):
"I freeze your love, I freeze your interest, I freeze our connection. You have no warmth for me, and I give none to you. Our bond is stopped, cold, and dead. It is done."

The Rest
Advanced Recipes

SECTION F: RETRIBUTION AND SEALING (4 Spells)

52. Instant Return Pouch
TOOLS: Mirror shard (reflective side out), Red pepper, Rue.

METHOD:
1. Place the mirror shard (reflective side facing outward), the red pepper (for fire/speed), and the Rue (for protection) into a small, black cloth bag.
2. Wear or carry this pouch at all times, especially when you feel targeted.
3. Visualize the mirror catching and bouncing back all incoming evil eye or negative energy.

COMMAND (Spoken over the pouch):
"I am protected, I am sealed. What is sent is instantly revealed. This pouch catches, turns, and returns all malice to the sender, threefold. My shield is iron. It is done."

53. Hot Foot Reversal
TOOLS: Chili powder, Sulphur powder (or black pepper), Red candle.

METHOD:
1. Mix the Chili powder and Sulphur/Black Pepper.
2. Write the sender's name on the red candle. Dress the candle with oil, pushing away from you.
3. Roll the candle in the powder. Light it and visualize the flame sending burning heat to the sender's feet, forcing them to flee their own attack.

COMMAND (Spoken while lighting the candle):
"You sent me heat, you receive an inferno. Your own fire burns your feet. Run from your creation, run from your mistake. The spell is seized and returned now. It is done."

The Rest
Advanced Recipes

54. The Uncrossing Bath
TOOLS: Hyssop (for cleansing), Epsom Salt, Lemon (juice or slices).

METHOD:
1. Draw a bath with hot water. Dissolve the Epsom Salt. Add the Hyssop and Lemon.
2. Submerge yourself fully. Focus on the water stripping away all foreign, negative, or cursed energies that cling to you.
3. Drain the tub and immediately shower in clean water, visualizing the last residue washing off you.

COMMAND (Spoken while in the bath):
"All crossed paths are straightened. All binds are broken. I am clean, uncrossed, and free from external influence. This curse is dissolved, this tie is cut. I am sovereign. It is done."

55. Iron Warding Box
TOOLS: Small iron box (for defense), Obsidian (for grounding/blocking), Black Salt.

METHOD:
1. Place the Obsidian stone and a heavy amount of Black Salt inside the iron box.
2. Seal the box tightly. Bury the box near your front door or keep it under your bed.
3. Visualize the iron and obsidian forming an unbreakable, permanent spiritual armor around your life.

COMMAND (Spoken as you seal the box):
"This is my fortress, strong and permanent. All evil, all malice, all attack is shattered upon this iron shield. No harm shall breach this defense. I am permanently sealed. It is done."

The Rest
Advanced Recipes

SECTION G: MANIPULATIVE LUST AND UNBREAKABLE BINDING (4 Spells)

56. Hot Desire Draw
TOOLS: Red candle, Cinnamon, Red thread.

METHOD:
1. Carve the target's name and a symbol of fire/passion onto the red candle.
2. Dress the candle with oil, pulling towards you. Roll it in Cinnamon (for heat and speed).
3. Wrap the red thread around the candle. Burn it down completely while visualizing the target's desire for you increasing to an unbearable level.

COMMAND (Spoken with heat):
"Your body burns for mine. Your mind seeks my touch. This fire commands your immediate, undeniable desire. You want me now, and you cannot resist. Draw to me swiftly. It is done."

57. Keep Him/Her True Bind
TOOLS: Two small dolls/poppets (representing yourselves), Red cord, Domination Oil.

METHOD:
1. Label the poppets (or attach photos). Dress them heavily with Domination Oil.
2. Tie the two poppets together tightly using the red cord, focusing on the unbreakable fidelity and devotion between you.
3. Store the bound dolls in a secure, dark place.

COMMAND (Spoken while binding):
"We are bound, sealed, and eternally true. Your heart belongs to me alone, and mine to you. No other will enter this sacred space. Our fidelity is unbreakable. It is done."

BeWitchy® Copyright © 2026 by Madame Verveine / The Devil's Crypt Pty Ltd / BeWitchy. All Rights Reserved.

The Rest
Advanced Recipes

58. Sweet Dreams Charm
TOOLS: Rose petals, Lavender, Brown sugar.

METHOD:
1. Mix the rose petals, lavender, and brown sugar into a small sachet or cloth bag.
2. Charge the sachet by focusing on the target having beautiful, sensual dreams about you.
3. Place the sachet under your mattress or pillow to send the dreams out every night.

COMMAND (Spoken over the sachet):
"In your sleep, you see my face. In your dreams, you feel my touch. All your subconscious desire is focused on me. You wake craving my presence. It is done."

59. Personal Magnetism Powder
TOOLS: Honey dust (or powdered sugar), Ginger (for power), Clove (for drawing).

METHOD:
1. Mix the Honey dust, Ginger, and Clove into a fine powder.
2. Hold the powder and visualize yourself as an irresistible magnetic force.
3. Lightly dust the powder onto your clothing, focusing on the collar, cuffs, or the bottoms of your shoes.

COMMAND (Spoken while applying):
"I am attraction. I am desire. All eyes turn toward my light. I draw compliments, opportunities, and affection everywhere I step. My presence is magnetic. It is done."

The Rest
Advanced Recipes

SECTION H: CURSES, HEXES, AND SPIRITUAL ATTACKS (5 Spells)

60. The Confusion Hex
TOOLS: Black pepper, Salt, Dirt, Paper with name.

METHOD:
1. Write the target's name nine times on the paper. Fold it away from you.
2. Mix the black pepper, salt, and dirt. Place the paper in the mix.
3. Place the container on a hard surface and bang it three times, commanding utter confusion in their life. Dispose of the mix far away.

COMMAND (Spoken while banging):
"Your mind is fogged, your thoughts are chaos. You cannot focus, you cannot decide, you cannot win. Every decision leads to error. Your life is confusion now. It is done."

61. Seven Days of Trouble
TOOLS: Seven Rusty Nails (for pain/failure), Cursing Oil (or Chili), Photo of Target (or name).

METHOD:
1. Dress the seven nails with the Cursing Oil.
2. Place the photo/name paper on a plate. Insert one rusty nail into the paper each day for seven days.
3. Each day, command a new type of trouble for the target (e.g., job loss, car trouble, argument).

COMMAND (Spoken daily):
"Day [Number]: I pierce your [specific area: luck/peace/health]. You will face trouble and failure now. This chain of chaos begins and cannot be stopped. It is done."

The Rest
Advanced Recipes

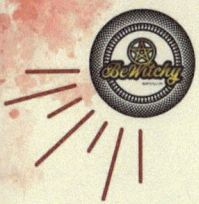

62. Financial Drain Jar
TOOLS: Vinegar, Old coins (stolen or found), Name on paper.

METHOD:
1. Write the target's name and their bank/business name on paper. Fold it away.
2. Place the paper and the old coins into the jar. Fill with vinegar (to sour their funds).
3. Shake the jar daily, commanding their accounts to drain and their expenses to explode.

COMMAND (Spoken while shaking):
"I sour your funds, I drain your wealth. Your money vanishes, your savings shrink. You will spend without reason and lose without gain. Poverty is your shadow now. It is done."

63. The Broken Mirror Curse
TOOLS: Shattered mirror pieces, Salt, Name of target.

METHOD:
1. Write the target's name on a paper and place it in the center of a cloth.
2. Place the shattered mirror pieces (facing upward) over the name. Cover with salt.
3. Wrap the cloth tightly. Command the shattering of their luck. Dispose of the package at a crossroads.

COMMAND (Spoken while wrapping):
"I shatter your good fortune. I break your reflection. Your luck is destroyed, your reputation fractured. You will find no peace or success. Curse begins now. It is done."

The Rest
Advanced Recipes

64. The Silence Bind
TOOLS: Black thread, Mouth-shaped paper (with name), Alum.

METHOD:
1. Cut the paper into the shape of a mouth. Write the target's name on it.
2. Sprinkle alum powder over the mouth. Fold it shut.
3. Wrap the mouth tightly with black thread until it is sealed. Bury or freeze the packet.

COMMAND (Spoken while binding):
"I sew your lips shut. I bind your malicious tongue. You cannot speak against me. You are silenced and sealed. Your words hold no power. It is done."

The Rest
Advanced Recipes

SECTION I: PETTY AND VENGEFUL MAGICK (2 Spells)

65. Lost Keys Hex
TOOLS: Salt, Paper with name, an old Key.

METHOD:
1. Write the target's name on the paper. Wrap the paper around the old key.
2. Place the wrapped key into a container and cover it completely with salt (to confuse the energies).
3. Shake the container daily, focusing on the target constantly losing important, everyday items.

COMMAND (Spoken while shaking):
"You search, but you do not find. The items you need are not where you look. Keys are lost, wallets disappear. Your life is minor frustration now. It is done."

66. The Perpetual Annoyance Switch
TOOLS: Rubber band, Small piece of aluminum foil (crinkled), Name of target.

METHOD:
1. Write the target's name on the foil. Crinkle it up into a tiny, annoying ball.
2. Wrap the rubber band around the foil ball repeatedly.
3. Keep the charm somewhere you can flick or snap the rubber band when you think of the target, sending them a small, sharp jolt of irritation.

COMMAND (Spoken while snapping the band):
"I am the source of your constant, tiny irritation. You are plagued by minor annoyances and inescapable frustration. Your peace is broken. The annoyance is perpetual. It is done."

The End:
The Final Command

You have reached the end of this journey, but the work—your work—is just beginning. You now hold the knowledge and the tools to protect your peace, claim your desires, and deal absolute justice to those who threaten you.

The Cunning Witch is not defined by external labels or historical traditions; you are defined by your results and your command.

The Final Command
- Own Your Power: You are the ultimate authority in your life. Never ask for permission to be powerful.
- Trust Your Will: Your spells work because you believe in them. Doubt is the only magic killer.
- Remember the Rule: Live with integrity and honor those who support you. But if anyone attempts to use their weakness or malice against you, remember what I told you in the beginning: you will always get the polar opposite!

Go forth and be the powerful, commanding Witch you were meant to be.

Madame Verveine

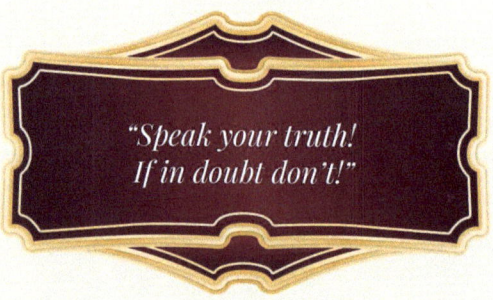

"Speak your truth! If in doubt don't!"

Spells Chapter 14: Case Files

Real stories related to the book.

Case Files:
Proof of the Work

Spells are words. Magick is action. These case files are here to prove that the principles—the polar opposite rule, the requirement for protection, and the absolute power of focused intent—are real. These are just a few examples of what happens when the Cunning Witch is in charge.

CASE FILE 1: THE EIGHT-YEAR OBSESSION (KARMA AND BOUNDARIES)

I once had a lady visit the BeWitchy shop in Australia asking for love spells. As we chatted, it became alarmingly clear she was the perennial third wheel. For eight long years, she had been obsessed with a man who had not only rejected her but had moved on, married, and started a new life. Even recently having a child with the new wife.

She openly admitted to me that she had continued to curse the new wife and harass the couple in a misguided bid to "win him back." The man was never hers; their relationship had dissolved long ago. She was cursing an innocent woman who had simply moved into a rightful, karmic place.

The Result: Despite her dedication, her entire life was ruined. She had nothing but bad luck, chaos, financial instability, and distress for the entire eight years she practiced this malicious magick. She couldn't see it, but her life was "ragged and shit" because she was fighting the tide and trying to steal happiness that was not her property.

The Lesson: Magick is a tool of justice and personal sovereignty, not delusion. If you fight what is karmically true—if you harm people who do not deserve it—the powers that be will ensure that your entire life suffers. If you use your power for something that isn't yours, it will turn everything you own to dust.

Case Files:
Proof of the Work

CASE FILE 2: THE BEWITCHY INCIDENT (PROOF OF THE POLAR OPPOSITE)

My company, BeWitchy, once faced a sustained and petty spiritual attack from a rival who was driven by pure, jealous malice. They initiated curses, public attacks, and spiritual binds against me and my business. They fully intended to destroy my reputation and close the doors on my success.

The Action Taken: I employed a combination of the Obsidian Mirror Box for constant reflection, the Freezer Banishing Spell to stop their actions, and the Reversal Candle Spell to send their own hateful energy back, amplified. I did not ask for new luck; I commanded the opposite of their intended outcome.

The Result: The rival's business collapsed rapidly. Their reputation was destroyed by their own actions and poor business choices. Simultaneously, BeWitchy saw an explosive surge in popularity, client volume, and media exposure. Every negative action they took resulted in an immediate, positive, and undeniable result for me.

The Lesson: When someone attacks a Cunning Witch, you don't just survive—you thrive. The energy they send becomes the fuel for your success. They wanted failure; they received it themselves, and I received the polar opposite of their desire: total, undeniable victory.

Case Files:
Proof of the Work

CASE FILE 3: THE FRAUDULENT CLIENT (INTEGRITY TEST)

I had a client attempt to cheat me out of a large fee for a custom working. They claimed the job was simple and tried to use various manipulation tactics, including false promises and outright lies about their financial situation, to pay far less than the agreed-upon price. This was a direct attack on my integrity and the value of my time.

The Action Taken: I immediately used a simple Go Away & Stay Away Road Opener combined with a targeted Sour Jar Curse. The spell wasn't just to remove them, but to ensure they faced the consequence of their dishonesty—financial hardship and inability to move forward with the money they'd held back.

The Result: Within a week, the client's own business suffered an unexpected, massive financial setback, far greater than the fee they attempted to avoid paying. Their planned projects stopped dead, and they were unable to secure new contracts.

The Lesson: Magick demands honesty. If you try to cheat the witch, you are cheating the universe. The consequences are swift and severe.

Always maintain your integrity, and the universe will enforce the lesson on those who lack theirs.

The End:
The Final Command

CASE FILE 4: THE BOARDROOM CONQUEST (DOMINATION SPELL)
A trusted client was facing a hostile takeover attempt that threatened to erase twenty years of their hard work. The opposing CEO was a known narcissist and extremely manipulative in negotiations, using fear and bullying to close deals. My client needed complete, dominating control of the meeting to secure their company's future.

The Action Taken: This was not a curse for chaos, but a spell for absolute authority. I executed a heavy Command Candle Spell using Purple wax and Domination Oil dressed in their favor. The client also performed the Success and Victory Wash immediately before entering the final negotiation, ensuring they radiated irrefutable dominance.

The Result: The client reported walking into the room with an almost physical shield of confidence. The opposing CEO, normally aggressive, became strangely passive, fumbling arguments and agreeing to terms they were previously sworn against. The client won the negotiation, kept their company, and secured a favorable, long-term deal.

The Lesson: Domination magick isn't just for love; it is the ultimate tool for career and financial sovereignty.
When you command, your will overrides the fear and doubt of others.
Always walk into a fight knowing you have already won.

Voodoo: Dolls

Pre-purchased Voodoo Dolls.
You can grab one of this link:
www.bewitchy.com

This little bad boy is all you need! That, intention, words, visualisation and she's done.

www.ingramcontent.com/pod-product-compliance
Lightning Source LLC
Chambersburg PA
CBHW042259280426
43661CB00108BA/1328/J